Brown on Brown:

The Autobiography of Jim E. Brown

Vol. 1: the Early Years

by Jim E. Brown

DEDICATION

To Darlene, Mildred, my Father, my Mum and my brother,
Mark F. Brown. And to myself, Jim E. Brown.

CONTENTS

ACKNOWLEDGMENTS

I couldn't have produced this book without all the teachers at Ashbury Meadow Primary School who taught me how to type. Typing this book was incredibly efficient. Had I wrote it out on loose-leaf pages it would have taken significantly longer to write.

1.) JIM E. BROWN, EAT YOUR PEAS!

I am 19 years old. Many people think I look older than 19 but due to a smattering of degenerative conditions I have the appearance of a 40-year-old.

Because of my appearance I was able to buy alcohol from a very early age (5), even though I've only been legally allowed to drink since I turned 18 last year. While the other youths at Ashbury Meadow Primary School were sipping on apple juice I was drinking Bellhaven Scottish Stout in the schoolyard. I suffer from alcoholism which has further aged me well beyond my 19 years.

My descent into alcoholism was both rapid and intense. My parents never discovered that I was hitting the bottle because I quickly learned how to hide it from them. For example, if my mum was making a jello, I'd pour a fifth of vodka into the water pitcher in our fridge just before she prepared it. You see, my mum made jello just about every day for me. I learned to feign appreciation for the gelatinous dessert, but in fact the nectar I truly desired was not made from pig hooves but fermented from potatoes...yes, Vodka!

I was 5 years old and buying the cheapest vodka money could buy on the daily. Where did a 5-year-old get the money to do this, you ask? Where there's a wall there's a way my friends; and no that's not a typo. I began panhandling by the wall near my house. Once I got the requisite five quid from strangers who felt bad for me I'd head right to Cradlebury Commons Market and purchase a plastic bottle of Nikita Imperial. Ah, the moment that clear liquid touched my tongue it was like heaven on earth.

But the fear of getting caught was too great. My older brother Mark F. Brown had been caught drinking a jug of wine behind the Tesco. My parents sent him off to a boarding school called Shacklebury Heights, an extremely rigid and difficult place for boys.

The Headmaster (Count Withersby) was notoriously cruel and would give each boy five lashes before bed as a matter of course. I knew I had to do whatever it took to avoid Shacklebury Heights. When Mark F. would come home for holiday he looked worn. The welts on his thighs were enormous and his joie de vivre had been sucked from him like a potato chip into a vacuum cleaner.

I was an alcoholic so I needed to keep drinking...but getting caught was not an option. After my mother prepared the jello each day I'd slip an Ambien into her lemonade and get blissfully twisted on booze as she slept. To ensure my father wouldn't catch me it was not so easy. You see, I feared slipping Ambien into his beverages as he had an Ambien Allergy.

He used to remind us all the time that Ambien gave him sores which would ooze pus. If he got enough of the pus-y sores on his face he could be fired from his job (he was a male model) and then the family wouldn't be able to afford canned bread and eggs to eat (my family loved canned bread...we used to eat canned brown bread for lunch and dinner each day and a boiled egg for breakfast). So, I had to find an alternate way to sedate him.

Even though I was only 5 years old I was very studious. I went to the John Ryland Library (on Deansgate) to study everything I could about anaesthetics. I was absolutely determined to find a way to sedate my father without creating those pus-y sores! learned about anaesthesiology. At the age of 6, after months of daily research, I began to sedate my father daily using a drug called Propofol which I stole from the Manchester Royal Infirmary (my Grandmother Petchula Clemmons worked there). Years later news broke of Pop Singer Mike Jackson and his untimely death due to Propofol abuse.

When I was five I looked 20. By the time I was 13 I looked over 30 years old. My adolescence was in its beginning stages and I was starting to take an interest in women. I would try to strike up conversations with extremely beautiful women in their 20s. When my appearance piqued their curiosity, the moment was almost always ruined by my high-pitched voice. You see, my balls hadn't dropped yet so I still had the innocent squeal of a pre-pubescent. It made women extremely uncomfortable. Every day I'd try to strike up a conversation with women as I rode the 23 Bus to my Didsbury Road stop. Finally, I met a woman who found the curious dissonance between my voice and my face appealing.

Her name was Carol Krathersburn, a divorced nurse from Droylsden. She was 47 at the time and lived with her two sons Edward and Joseph, 13 and 14. Little did she know that I was also a student at Ashbury Meadows, just like her boys. When she took me home with her I had no idea they were her sons. I knew the repercussions of Ed and Joe finding out about this affair would be too dire for me to deal with. Luckily my expertise in anaesthesiology came in handy. I sedated them (and their mother) with the Propofol and IV I had in my knapsack and rushed off.

When I got home mum had prepared a spread of 2 loaves of canned bread on the table. Dad and I started furiously pounding the bread down our gullets. It felt good to eat after the stress of sedating my classmates but what I really needed was a shot of vodka. The only problem was I had used my day's rations of propofol so I wouldn't be able to sedate Dad. Should I just tell him I was an alcoholic? No, not worth the risk of being sent to Shacklebury Heights like Mark F.

"Dad." I said. "What's it like being a male model?"

"Well, Jim E.," said Dad "being a male model is kind of like eating a loaf of bread. It's nourishing in that it provides money for the family but it's rewarding in that it tastes good."

"But how can modelling have a taste?" I asked.

"Well, it doesn't literally taste good, but if it were a food, it would taste good."

"I don't understand Dad."

"In time you will, Jim E., in time you will."

My father patted me on the head and pinched my cheek.

"Don't you want to go to bed, Dad?"

"It's only 5pm Jim...and my bed time isn't until 7:30"

"Ah. Ok. But maybe it's better if you go to bed a little earlier than that?"

"Why would that be, Jim?"

"No reason." I said. My mind was racing. I was dying for a fix. I'd need to figure out a way to get at least a little booze on my tongue or the shaking would begin and then my parents would certainly learn about my drinking problem.

I looked at my father's face. I knew the only way I could get him to sleep was with an Ambien. The thought of those pus-y boils ruining his male modelling career sent a chill through my spine but I couldn't resist. I slipped an Ambien into his evening glass of milk and he went out like a light. "Easy as pie" I thought to myself as I gulped down a fifth of vodka.

In the morning I was awoken by a shriek. It was my father. I ran upstairs. He was in the bathroom staring at a face covered in pus-y boils. "Today's my big shoot! I'll have to cancel! My career is over!" He began to weep. "I didn't take an Ambien! And that's the only way these pus-y boils appear! How could an Ambien have been placed into my system?"

I said nothing. My father was a trusting man, and he couldn't imagine that his own son would betray him this way. He didn't know the depths of my alcoholism. There was a lot he didn't know.

My father took his own life minutes later. From that day forward my mother became the breadwinner. She took up a job as a teller at Coutts & Co. bank on Hardman Blvd.

But even though she was the breadwinner, we would never eat bread again. It reminded her too much of Dad.

From that day forward we ate only peas in the Brown household.

2.) ROSIE

When I was 17 (in 2017) I had a massive crush on a girl at my secondary school, Barlow RC High School in East Didsbury. Her name was Rosie Roberts.

Rosie was the finest that East Didsbury had to offer. It was love at first site. She was new to Barlow RC and had transferred from CHS in Chorlton-cum-Hardy.

If only those Chorlton-cum-Hardy boys knew what they were missing out here in East Didsbury. Rosie had it all; beauty, brains and charm. I knew she was the one for me when we sat next to each other in British History. While elderly and frail Mr. Jones prattled on about Lord Beaconsfield and William Gladstone I would pass her notes on little pieces of paper. I was too shy to tell her my true feelings, so I'd write things like "Hey" or "Hi" or "What's up?"

When she'd write back I'd get too shy to respond and I'd ask Mr. Jones for permission to go to the WC. He must have thought I had a bladder infection or IBS considering how much I used that bathroom. I promised myself I'd tell Rosie my true feelings one day, but I missed my opportunity. You see, Rosie's father got a job at a cracker factory in Berwick-upon-Tweed all the way in Northumberland in May of 2017 and she disappeared.

After she left I deeply regretted that I had never been honest with her about my feelings. I scrambled to find her contact information but she must have been going by an alias on Facebook...I couldn't find her. I called every cracker factory in town to see if a Mr. Roberts had started working as the foreman but to no avail. Had she lied to me? Or did her dad have a different name?

When I obsessed over Rosie it helped distract me from thoughts of my father's untimely death. I was haunted by the image of his pus-y boils. I became desperate. I had no money but I would figure out a way to get to Berwick-upon-Tweed. I could take the Transpennine Express and transfer to the CrossCountry Edinburgh. But the train to York alone would cost 30 pounds. I considered riding my bike there, but it would have taken 19 hours, which was time I didn't have. I was in love and needed to see Rosie.

I went to Coutts & Co. to find me mum. "Mum," I said. "I need a ride to Berwick-upon-Tweed."
"Berwick-upon-Tweed?" she said. "That's at least a 4-hour drive if we take the M6! Why in the world would you need to go there?"
"Mom, I'm in love."
"In Love you say? With who?
"Her name is Rosie Roberts and she was the most beautiful girl in all of East Didsbury!"
Mum paused.
"Look Jim E., I know what it feels like to be in love. Your father was the greatest man I've ever known and being in a loving marriage with him was the most rewarding and profound thing that has ever happened to me. I miss him every day."

I felt a pang of guilt knowing that I had been partially responsible for Dad's untimely death. How could Mom ever know that I slipped him the Ambien that caused all those pus-filled boils on his face to appear?

"It's alright Mum, you don't need to give me a ride."

"No, Jim E., I have to. Love is too important to let it slip away just because this girl moved to Berwick-upon-Tweed. Let's go. I'll drive you there right away!"

I felt guilty because poor Mum would never know my secret. But I longed for Rosie too badly.

Mum's boss Mr. Smothfeld saw her gathering her belongings. "Mrs., Brown, are you leaving early?"

"Yes Mr. Smothfeld, it's a family emergency."

"I understand completely Mrs. Brown. Godspeed." He looked at me for a second, then back at my mum. He winked at her.

As we drove on M61 Mum asked all kinds of questions about Rosie. What she was like, her interests, her aspirations, her family. The truth was I didn't know anything. I tried to change the subject. "So, Mr. Smothfeld seems nice." I said.

"Mr. Smothfeld and I are just friends!" she responded, shocked.

I hadn't suspected anything between Mum and Smothfeld. But her suspicious retort made me think there was something going on. I kept quiet about it.

After some time we arrived in Berwick-upon-Tweed. Now I could be reunited with my lovely Rosie! But first I needed to eat. I was

famished. I had Mum drive to the McDonalds on Loaning Meadows.
I was nearly broke so I ordered a Quarter Pounder but without
cheese, meat, mayo, ketchup, lettuce or anything else. Just the bun for
me.

First I scraped the sesame seeds off and placed them in my pocket to
snack on later. Then I took a bite. That glorious bread filled me with
a feeling of hope. I just knew I'd find Rosie.

But across from the McDonalds I noticed a Cineplex which was
playing *Thor: Raganrok*. First, I'd go see the film, then I'd look for
Rosie.

"But I thought you wanted to find your sweetheart dear Jim E.! Not
see a film!" said Mum.

After much deliberation she agreed to wait in the car while I watched
Thor: Raganrok. I walked into the theatre and lo and behold...there
stood Rosie behind the concession stand. I walked up to her, slowly,
in disbelief.

"Rosie" I said.
"Did you go to Barlow RC in East Didsbury?" she said.
"Yes..."
"Wow! What a coincidence! What brings you to Berwick-upon-
Tweed?" she said
I was speechless. I didn't know what to do or what to say. My gut
feeling was to run away. I darted towards the exit. Then I
remembered my entire mission had been to find Rosie. And here she
was. "TURN BACK AROUND!" I told myself.

With every ounce of strength in my body I willed myself back to the
concession stand.

"Are you alright?" said Rosie?

I didn't know what to do or what to say. The only thing I could think of was to let her know I had just bought a bun from McDonalds. I pulled the sesame seeds from my pocket and offered them to her. "Fresh from the bun!" I said.

Rosie chuckled awkwardly. "Here, why don't you have some popcorn on me?" she said.

I watched her beautiful frame scoop a heaping pile of popped corn into a paper bag. Then she began to spritz the corn with a hot yellowed butter. She passed the bag to me and smiled. I nearly fainted. I was too nervous to say anything to her, even a thank you. Plus, I'd always heard girls liked brash bullies more than gentlemen. So, I didn't thank her for the corn. I just walked away.

I had never tried popcorn before and wasn't really interested in it. I dumped it in the closest dustbin I could find (out of Rosie's sight).

I sat through *Thor: Raganrok* and unsurprisingly it was masterful. I found a Fire Exit in the back of the theatre so I could avoid seeing Rosie. I found Mum in the car. She was FaceTiming with Mr. Smothfeld.

My life was at a standstill. I didn't know what would happen between Rosie and I, between Mum and Smothfeld. I didn't know if anyone would ever find out I had slipped Dad the pus-y boil inducing Ambien. Or if Mark F. would ever return from Shacklebury Heights.

3.) MY FIRST FLING WITH DARLENE

The love of my life, Darlene Viglianco is a human and I respect her immensely for that. In the age of cellular phones, desktop and laptop computers, WiFi and the like it can be immensely moving just to touch a warm bit of human flesh. No matter how much comfort we get from iPhone 10s and 11s, they will never resonate the way the warm and hairy skin covering your lover's flesh, blood and organs will. I miss Darlene every day.

Darlene and I first met at Greedy's Fish & Chips in Upper Swell. I was in that remote region to escape what was becoming an oppressive situation with my mother. Her affair with Mr. Smothfeld was out in the open and the very thought of seeing a man besides my father kiss her made me swell with anger.

My drinking was out of control because of the stress. I was pounding a fifth of standard Nikita Imperial Vodka for breakfast. I had discovered that if I ate more food I could manage to drink even more alcohol. So, after my morning fifth of Vodka I'd make myself 6 boiled eggs. Sometimes I'd eat each whole, one by one, or if I was in a rush I'd blend them into a smoothie in the old Vitamix and drink them out of a coffee mug. Then I'd follow it up with a round of Red Bull Vodkas at Ye Olde Cock, the finest pub in all of East Didsbury.

I was a regular at Ye Olde Cock. I loved drinking myself into a stupor there. I can't tell you how many times the old barkeep Anton Wilson had to clean vomit, diarrhoea and urine from the floor because of me. Every day I'd go in, order a Red Bull Vodka and a piece of bread. I'm a rather picky eater and one of the few things I like to eat beside eggs is bread. Typically, my family would eat eggs for breakfast and bread for lunch and dinner. I prefer canned bread to fresh.

Since the untimely death of my father, my mother had insisted on making only peas for Dinner, and no Bread. I couldn't stand the taste of peas. I grew to hate my mother deeply for this alone, but when she began her affair with Smothfeld it was the final straw. I had to escape to Upper Swell, at least for a while. Yes, I'd miss East Didsbury and Ye Olde Cock, but sometimes self-care means taking yourself out of toxic environments.

Smothfeld's presence in my home felt like a slap in the face to the memory of my father, who died with pus-y boils all over his face. Imagine a face covered with pus-y boils being smacked...the pus would explode everywhere! Smothfeld clearly had no conception of how vile and perverse he truly was. I suspect he's a sociopath.

Around this time I became rather fond of a candy called Gushers. As I said before, I'm not one for experimenting with different foods and such. Bread and eggs is enough for me. But Gushers were interesting. They were gelatinous on the outside, but when you bit into them you'd get a hot spurt of sweet & sour liquid. The sensation was thrilling to say the least.

Maybe I'm a masochist, but I think the Gushers reminded me of my father's pus-filled boils. When he had a poke at one of those rotund boils it would leak a goopy load of pus, much like the juice of a Gusher. It took three years of psychotherapy to come to this realization.

I was drinking my 8th Diet Pepsi and Whisky at Greedy's Fish and Chips. My tummy was full of Diet Pepsi, Eggs, Whiskey, Bread and Gushers. I guess I overwhelmed my system because I projectile vomited across the entire bar. I saw chunklets of boiled egg yolk, and the gelatinous white membrane, all coated with Gushers liquid flying across the bar.

One little egg chunklet landed on a brown-haired bombshell, Darlene.

I had never seen anyone like her. 5 foot 3, around 13 stone and dressed in a pink hooded sweatshirt and loose-fitting jeans. She was the image of perfection. Forget Rosie or any of the others.

Darlene was disgusted by the scrap of vomit which landed on her. She instinctively began to vomit herself. I closely observed the content of her vomit. I saw the unmistakable sign of Gusher remnants in the putrid liquid she had expelled.

She collapsed to the floor. I used it as an opportunity to inspect her vomit more thoroughly. I saw what appeared to be boiled egg yolk remnants as well. Was this woman eating the same diet as I was? I began to shake her. "WAKE UP! WAKE UP!" I screamed.

She slowly opened her eyes. She had vomit dribbling from her mouth, as did I. "I'm sorry I vomited on you, but I was wondering, miss...have you been eating Gushers and Eggs?"

She took a moment to gather her bearings. She seemed confused, and responded slowly. "Why, yes, those are some of the only things I eat."

"And me as well!" I shouted aloud. Normally I wouldn't be so forward but the Diet Pepsi Whiskys must have lowered my inhibitions.

"Can I kiss you?" I said.

"Yes!" she shouted emphatically, without hesitation.

We frenched for the better part of an hour, rolling around in the pools of our respective vomit. She attempted to touch my private sack, but as I'm a gentleman I'd never allow that on a first date.

"What's your name?" I said

"Darlene" she said.

"The moment of intimacy we just shared was far more healthy and less toxic than anything Mother would do with Smothfeld." I said.

"I don't understand" said Darlene.

"I'll tell you all about it at a later time."

The day I met Darlene would be the first day of the rest of my life.

4.) PHISH IS MY FAVORITE BAND AND THE TIME I LOST MY VIRGINITY TO DARLENE

Phish, in addition to being some of the finest musicians and songwriters of the 20th Century, also have a devout following and a wonderful online forum called Phantasy Tour. I spent many years of my youth lurking the depths of the Phantasy Tour forum. The contributors there made me into the man I am today. It would seem that many of them had substance abuse issues and possible undiagnosed mental health disorders. Since I had been abusing alcohol from the age of five, I felt a real kinship with these Phish Phanatics.

I remember one night, I was 12 years old. It was late. My parents were fast asleep and I was rather sloshed from a bottle of Nikita Imperial I had devoured. It had been a rough day. My father had come home from his male modelling gig in a wretched mood. His therapist had prescribed him Lexapro which he found helpful. But he was off his meds for the day. Once he got home, he sat in the corner screaming and crying. If anyone came within feet of him he'd scream blood murder. "What's wrong Dad?" I said.

"Get the fuck away from me you creep!" he yelled. I got a glimpse of his face. It was covered with pus filled boils. When I looked at the ground there was a pool of pus there. He must have been scratching at his boils because he was in a depressive mood. I saw little droplets of blood in the pus too.

It was stressful for my entire family, but my coping mechanism was alcohol and Phantasy Tour. I couldn't admit it to myself at the time, but the Phish Forum was a passive aggressive outlet for me to disparage other users in order to feel better about my problems at home. I did genuinely love Phish, but it seemed that I only felt good about myself when I was bringing others down. This is in no way the right thing to do, but it was what I did.

Looking back, it was transference plain and simple. For example, I was embarrassed that my Dad was a male model and I was embarrassed by his pus-filled boils and sores. So, I'd criticise other Phish fans on Phantasy Tour for the same thing. I'd make a thread and say "I THINK BLAZEONTWEEZER'S DAD HAS PUS FILLED BOILS!" Or "I THINK PSYCHOKILLER666'S DAD IS A GAY MALE MODEL." Somehow, I never realized I was referring to my own situation.

I always hoped that Phish would tour the UK and come to Manchester. I had a fantasy that I'd meet Trey at a pub in East Didsbury and that he'd do an impromptu set for a small crowd. But Phish never came to Manchester and I never saw any of the guys at any of the pubs in East Didsbury. When I heard Trey was sober I knew I'd never meet my hero at a pub. It was one of the real reasons I began writing my music. If I can go on tour, maybe just maybe one day I'll get to meet Phish out on the road. Usually they don't have opening acts but maybe they'd let me, Jim E. Brown open up for them.

But enough about Phish. Let me tell you about losing my virginity to Darlene on a beach. We were both wildly intoxicated. I had imbibed a medley of marijuana, Percocet and Red Bull Vodkas…and I had saved a bit of cocaine to freebase when we arrived at Formby Point, Merseyside. Darlene and I had been seeing each other on and off for a few months now. After we saw boiled eggs in each other's vomit at the bar we had struck up an intimate relationship. We could kiss and cuddle but I wasn't emotionally prepared to penetrate yet. Darlene was rather insistent upon it. The whole thing made me nervous so I made sure to intoxicate myself heavily to take the edge off.

We drove up to Formby Point. "This will be romantic, Jim E."
Darlene said.
I felt the knot in my stomach tighten. I farted very loudly. Too much boiled eggs for breakfast (I stress eat, which is why I am obese, but more on that later).
Darlene laughed at my flatulence, which hurt my feelings and

offended me deeply. "Fuck you bitch! You're just like the rest of them!" I screamed. I began to passionately freebase my cocaine as I cried. They say sticks and stones can break my bones but words will never hurt me. But Darlene's words hurt worse than even the largest boulder. Shouldn't she know that I'm sensitive about my flatulence?
"I'm sorry, Jim E., I didn't mean…"
"You didn't mean what?" I screamed. 'You didn't mean to show how much of a conniving SNAKE you are?"
"Don't talk to me that way Jim!"

Darlene got out of the car. She tripped on a seashell in the parking lot. She landed flat on her face and blood began to leak from her. She farted. I began to laugh uncontrollably. She got up.
"See Jim E.! You laughed at me!"
"It was not the same at all, Darlene!" I said.

Her bloodied face reminded me of the pus-y bloody face my Dad had. Maybe I've always been subconsciously attracted to my father (He was a handsome male model after all), but I felt so turned on by all this. "Let's make love, Darlene!" I said.

We tip-toed through the sand and stripped until we were naked. I had no idea how any of this sex business worked, but Darlene was an expert. She gave very clear and precise instructions on how to properly place my erect penis into her vaginal cavity. Once that occurred I thrusted back and forth (as she instructed) and eventually ejaculated. It was a very enjoyable experience.

5.) MY TRIP TO SHACKLEBURY HEIGHTS

No one wants to be lonely, least of all me. But I've experienced loneliness repeatedly. I remember when my brother Mark F. Brown was caught behind the Tesco with a jug of wine and sent off to the dreaded Shacklebury Heights. I was very close with Mark F. Every morning we'd boil our eggs together then walk to school and get into mischief. He's the reason I became an alcoholic as he introduced me to Bellhaven Scottish Stout at the age of 5. When the Headmaster of Schacklebury Heights dragged him from our home it was the saddest day of my life. The image of his tear stained face pleading to stay home will be forever burned into my memory.

One day I decided I'd try to visit him at Shacklebury Heights. I knew no visitors were allowed so I devised an intricate plan. Due to degenerative conditions I looked to be in my twenties when I was five. I dressed up as a cafeteria worker and snuck on the premises. I witnessed first-hand all the horrors that Shacklebury Heights had to offer. The stories were true; it was as hellish as imaginable. Boys from the ages of 7-12 tied up with chains and locked in cells. This looked more like a prison then a school. I made my way to the cafeteria and snuck into the Kitchen. They were preparing a gruel made from pig hooves, eggs, flour and condensed milk. After stewing the slop for 8 hours they'd garnish it with vitamin and mineral tablets. This was all the boys at Shacklebury Heights ever got to eat.

Lunch Lady Grizelda Walters saw me. "Who in fuck's name are you?" She shouted. I could smell the cigarettes and brandy on her breath. "I'm new here. Jim E...." I realized I couldn't give my real name. I didn't want Mark F. to get in trouble. "Jim E. Walters is my name, I'm new."

"Walters? Why that's my last name too!" Said Lunch Lady Grizelda Walters. "Well, you distribute the slop to the children Jim E. Each boy gets one ladle full of slop. After you ladle the slop in the bowl sprinkle the vitamin and mineral tablets on top."

"No problem Grizelda!" I said. She looked at me longingly for a moment. "After you're done come to my office. I want to speak with you."

I began distributing ladles of slop to every child in line, just waiting for my brother Mark F. Over 10,000 unfortunate boys lived at Shacklebury Heights. Each child looked sadder than the next. After 6 hours of ladling slop, I finally caught a glimpse of Mark F. He was now 10 years old but he looked solemn and aged. He had a black eye and was shaking nervously. I locked eyes with him. For a moment he looked excited to see me. But the trauma of being punished by the staff of Shacklebury Heights had given him a severe case of PTSD. He was abused and incapable of sharing even a brief moment of time with me for fear of retribution. When it came to be his turn I ladled the slop in his bowl but I topped it off with two hard boiled eggs which I had kept in my pocket, our favourite breakfast treat. He darted his eyes nervously around and quickly gulped both eggs down without chewing. He nodded to me and walked off. So that was all I'd see of my brother, the person I adored more than anyone in the world. I felt deeply saddened, but I knew I had to pay due diligence to Lunch Lady Grizelda Walters before exiting the premises.

I stepped into her office. She was wearing lingerie, which I had expected.
But I wasn't expecting that she'd be dead. Her fleshy round belly protruded from the scant lingerie as she lay in a pool of her own blood. Her head was caved in. And in her left hand was a hammer. I shrieked in horror. I had never seen a dead body before. On the table was a note. Handwritten.

It said "Dear Jim E., I waited all afternoon for you but I couldn't wait any longer. Too many men have stood me up, so I have decided to take my own life. I'm going to smash my skull in with a hammer. If you're reading this note it means you did come to see me, and didn't stand me up and my death was in vain. Love, Lunch Lady Grizelda Walters"

I was shaken. I had barely known Lunch Lady Grizelda Walters but her death was untimely. I felt lonely living in a world without her. I shed a tear. My single tear drop landed in her pool of blood like rain in a puddle. I vowed never to return to Shacklebury Heights.

6.) WHEN DARLENE AND I SPLIT

I've had trouble with my weight for my entire life. Too many eggs and too much liquor and wine has made me obese.

When I was 14 I was a rotund sack of flesh. I'd spend my days drinking Bellhaven Scottish Stout and Nikita Imperial Vodka and eating loads of boiled eggs and brown loaves of bread from the can. I'd spend my evenings reading all about Phish on the Phantasy Tour forums. I imagine many of my Phish loving cohort were as obese as me. I imagined all of us rolling around in a room together nude, our fat flesh bobbing up and down in a communal ritual in celebration of the human body.

But that was just a fantasy. The truth was that I sat looking at Phantasy Tour crying bitter tears. One reason I hate crying is that my tears taste like shit. I'm sure that many of the regular contributors to Phantasy Tour spend lots of time crying. And there's nothing wrong with that.

I remember after witnessing the brutal suicide of Lunch Lady

Grazelda Walters I would cry daily. She smashed her own head in with a hammer and that wasn't a very pretty sight. The Headmaster, Dean Withersby couldn't have cared less about the death of one his most valuable employees.

Lunch Lady Grazelda Walters had been preparing the slop at Shacklesbury Heights for 36 years, but of course he replaced her within a day. Lunch Lady Grazelda Walters was chubby herself. I wonder if she felt stigmatized by society's insistence that women be petite with Barbie-like figures. My father was always rail thin (a male model), but he had pus-filled boils that would appear on his face as an allergic reaction to drugs like Ambien.

Darlene never took umbrage with my weight. She was also rather thick, just like me. She had a penchant for eating eggs and Gushers, just like me. My third food of choice is Canned Brown Bread. But Darlene's third food of choice was Crabcakes. She loved a good Crabcake. I remember once taking her out to eat at Dmitris Tapas Taverna in East Didsbury. They didn't serve Crabcakes or Gushers or Eggs or Canned Bread. What a shithole. We ended up ordering two cocktails (Redbull Vodka) just to be polite. But we got in a big fight that night.

Darlene said that she never understood the appeal of Phish.
"You're kidding, right?" I said, concerned.
"I mean, maybe they're ok...it just seems their music is a bit meandering is all." Darlene responded.
I instinctively flipped the table over. Patrons from the other tables at the restaurant looked frightened.
Darlene shrieked.
"Shut the fuck up!" I yelled.

Darlene ran off. I watched her disappear down Liverpool Road.

I could have chased after her. I could have called her. I could have texted. I could have done something, anything.

But I did nothing. That was the last time I'd ever see Darlene. And to this day I still regret yelling at her. I lost the love of my life in an argument over Phish. Was it worth it?

No, no it was not.

7.) MEETING MILDRED

Now that I'm 19 I have experienced a plethora of emotions. I've loved and I've lost. After Darlene and I got into that big fight about Phish I didn't think I would ever be able to love again. I regretted my immature behaviour. I vowed to treat my next lover with compassion, dignity and respect.

Carol Ann Duffy was the very first female Poet Laureate of the United Kingdom and she lived not too far from me in West Didsbury (I'm from East Didsbury). I nearly shit my pants when I found out someone so prominent lived so close by. I was quite intoxicated when I found out; I had already had 5 Bellhaven Scottish Stouts and a few shots of a good Whiskey. But it was only 2pm so I knew the Beswick Library on Grey Mare Ln would still be open. I walked through the door and approached an elderly woman standing behind a desk.

"Where's your Carol Ann Duffy section?" I said to her.
"We don't have a Carol Ann Duffy section" she said.
"Fuck off! I'll go to the Manchester Bookery and pay good money for one of her books then. I should have listened when Mum said

nothing in life comes free!"

I spat in the librarian's face and turned around.

"Wait!" she yelled. I turned around "Sir, I don't think you understand how libraries work. You see, we don't have a whole section devoted to just one author. We use the Dewey Decimal system to sort our books!"

I didn't understand what this batshit crazy woman was talking about. "Look, lady, can you get me a Carol Ann Duffy book or no?"

"Let me check." she said.

"Ah, yes, we do have some of her material. Follow me!"

I started to feel guilty about having spit in her face. She hadn't bothered to wipe it off so a thick slimy stream of my saliva was still making its way down her nose.

"Look, miss, I apologize for yelling and spitting," I said. "I'm quite intoxicated. You see, I'm an alcoholic. I think I still feel mad about losing the love of my life, Darlene when we got into an argument about Phish."

"It's alright dearie" the old lady said.

"You have spittle on your face. May I wipe it off for you?" I said.

She consented. I took the lapel of my trench coat and wiped her face. Being this close to the librarian forced me to look into her eyes. She was actually quite attractive.

"Thanks," she said.

"What's your name?" I said.

"Mildred Browning" she said.

"Browning? Why, my surname is Brown!" I said.

She showed me the Carol Ann Duffy selection but I was already disinterested in that. I was more interested in Mildred Browning.

"Look Mildred, thanks for finding the book for me but I'm realizing now that I don't feel like reading it. But look, could I take you out for dinner tonight?"

Mildred paused.

"I'm married" she said.

"FUCK THAT!" I yelled. When I yell, and in general, I have a very antagonistic and threatening facial structure. I think Mildred felt scared.

"I..I..I'm married, but we could still have dinner. It's not like it means anything."
"Right, I said. Ye Olde Cock Tavern at 3pm?"

"3pm, that's a bit early for dinner, isn't it? And besides it's already past 3pm now."
"Oh fuck it, when do you get off work Mildred?"
"I'm off at 5."
"I'll see you at Ye Olde Cock at 5 then" I said.

That 1 hour and 40 minutes waiting for Mildred to meet me at Ye Olde Cock were some of the longest minutes of my life. But at 5:08 she walked through the door and all was well.

Mildred looked through the menu. "I think I'll just have a side of peas, I'm not very hungry" she said.

Peas? Peas? My mother always fed me peas. I never liked the taste of peas. But that's all she'd feed us after Father died. I was offended and disgusted by Mildred's menu selection. It actually hurt my feelings a bit. To cope I popped a Gusher into my mouth. The exploding thick innards of the Gusher reminded me of my Father's pus-filled boils.

The waiter came. I ordered my usual, a Red Bull Vodka and some bread. Mildred ordered a Pinot Noir and a side of peas.

8.) MILDRED MOVES IN

Mildred left her husband shortly after we dined at Ye Olde Cock. He was a sad sack and their marriage had been on the rocks for years. His name was Reginald Browning and he worked at the Stockport Sewage Works as a labourer. So, it didn't come as a surprise to anyone, least of all me when she left. I could tell Mildred was pining for my love. She moved into the flat on Brassington Rd. near the Stockport Sewage Works with mum and I.

Mildred and Mum bonded over their shared love of peas. Every day at supper time they'd boil or roast a big pot of them and gobble them up. I found this behaviour repulsive but I loved Mildred and I forgave her. After supper the gals would have a bowl of Creamed Ice, either strawberry, chocolate or Rum & Raisin. When I was a youth I loved a good Creamed Ice. Mark F. and I would beg mum to take us to the Mr. Whippy on Bexhill Rd. for a Creamed Ice. Typically she'd say no but every so often she'd consent (when Dad had a particularly fruitful male modelling session) and Mark F. and I would jump for joy.

Mum and Mildred were both slim and trim even though they ate Creamed Ice on the regular. I suppose eating peas exclusively creates a caloric deficit which affords one the opportunity to eat Creamed Ice and never get fat. I was fat as ever. My drinking had gone into overdrive and I was eating 8-12 loaves of canned bread per day. I suppose our home needed some fat to balance out the thin.

I look back fondly on this time in my life. Watching Mildred and Mum eat those peas was disgusting but it was nice to be surrounded by women who loved me. Both were the same age, the only difference being that Mildred would fuck me and that's not something I'd ever do with Mum.

Life was easy and pleasant. Each day Mom would go to Coutts & Co. and Mildred would go to Beswick Library at around 7:30. I'd usually be in bed, sleeping off a night of heavy drinking at Ye Olde Cock. I'd typically wake up around 1pm, eat a loaf or two of canned bread, have a few Bellhaven Scottish Stouts and maybe work on my poetry or just watch tele.

One day, at around 9am I believe, Mildred and Mum were already gone and I heard a knock at the door. I slowly got out of bed and answered the door. It was the last person I wanted to see: Reginald Browning, Mildred's ex.

I knew he was a labourer at the Stockport Sewage Works, but I didn't realize that that would be so blatantly obvious just looking at him. He was wearing coveralls which were splattered with massive chunks of faecal matter. He reeked of sewage.

"What do you want, fuck?"

I was angry that he deigned to step foot on my property.

"I'm sorry, Jim E.," his head dropped and he began to cry.

He really was a sad sack. I couldn't believe Mildred had wasted her youth with him. "I would never come by here if it wasn't an emergency. Is Mildred around?"

"Mildred is mine now, cock!" I yelled.

"Sorry, Jim E.! It's just, well, I have some bad news that I thought it best to relay in person."

He looked at me with pleading eyes. His eyelids were stained with faeces.

"Well, Reg, if there's something you need to tell Mildred you can tell me. And I'll relay the message."

"Very well Jim. Well, I...I...I was trying to be nice to my and Mildred's son Al. I got him a job at the Stockport Sewage Works. It was going grand. He was learning to be a man and make a living for himself!"

"This is the news you brought me, Reg? Fuck off."

"No, Jim, that's not the end of it. Al, he...he fell into a pool of wastewater. He drowned in the faecal matter. He's...dead!" Reg began to weep like a child.

"Alright, Reg. I'm sorry to hear that. I'll let Mildred know."

"Thank you for your kindness Jim!" Reg tried to lean in for a hug but I shooed him away. I watched him walk down the road as the smell of faeces began to dissipate.

I considered telling Mildred about the death of her son Al but I decided against it. Why ruin a good vibe with bad news?

9. A TRIP TO THE UNITED STATES

Mildred was a loving woman but I was becoming disillusioned with her. I felt a bit guilty that I hadn't told her about her son drowning in faeces. But overall, I was dissatisfied sexually.

It was clear that her love of peas fuelled my interest in her because it subconsciously reminded me of Mum. The whole situation was getting heavy for me. I decided to save up a few quid and travel to the US.

I had always been fond of American music and my tinned bread of choice is also American. I decided to visit the B&M Bread Canning factory in Portland, Maine.

I flew into Boston airport and took the Amtrak Downeaster to Portland. I got to try a selection of American beers on the train. Stone IPA and Bud Light were my favourites. They tasted nothing like my beloved Bellhaven Scottish Stouts but they got me sufficiently sloshed...which was a pleasant respite from the stress of travel and living with Mildred.

I arrived in Portland and booked a room at the Sandpiper Beachfront
Motel on Peaks Island. I don't care for beaches in the least. I find the
smell of that salty water repulsive. It reminds me of seafood, which I
refuse to eat. The only thing I eat is canned bread and boiled eggs for
breakfast. Occasionally I'll eat Gushers, but only because the bursting
sensation of chewing on one resonates with me because of the
memory of my father's pus-filled boils.

I checked into my room and immediately closed the blinds so I
wouldn't have to look at the disgusting ocean or the sickening sandy
beach. I was feeling famished. I called the front desk and asked if they
could bring up some canned B&M Bread. They said they didn't have
that in their kitchen. I found this shocking as I had assumed all of
New England would be a veritable canned bread utopia. I guess I was
wrong.

I walked to Hannigan's Island Market and found a few loaves. They
had only one can of Brown Bread and several cans of Brown Bread
with raisins. I don't prefer the raisin variety but I snatched them up
anyway. You can never be too careful. I picked up a 12 pack of Bud
Light which I was quickly developing a taste for. I drank 10 of them
and had a peaceful sleep.

I woke up the next morning at 2pm. I knew the B&M Factory
wouldn't be open all day so I had to get a move on. I quickly downed
my last two Bud Lights then headed for the Ferry. I got on the boat
and my senses were assaulted for the better part of an hour by the
grotesque odour of the Ocean. It took all the strength I had not to
vomit.

After two hours of travel on the Ferry and two buses   I arrived at the
B&M Factory. It looked like any other factory you might see in
Manchester from the exterior. It made me feel warm and cosy inside
because it reminded me of home. Maybe I was beginning to miss
Mildred and Mum and their plates of peas and bowls of Creamed Ice.

I didn't have an appointment at the factory. I read online that getting
a tour was near impossible. I figured I'd try my luck. I snuck round
back to the loading dock and saw a freight truck pulling up. I hopped
on the back of it and rode in. I was extremely nervous about getting
caught. This was most certainly trespassing. So, I was breaking the
law in a foreign country. Not only that, I was starting to get the
shakes because I only had two beers in me.

"I'm fucked!" I thought to myself as I walked into the depths of the
factory. It seemed like a panic attack might be setting in. But then my
nostrils were exposed to the scent of freshly steamed canned bread,
and all my troubles started to melt away. I saw huge vats of brown
liquid. Tubes spraying brown liquid. Hot steam. This was "where the
magic happens."

I was in a reverie. I began stumbling around the factory without a
care. No one seemed to notice me. I saw a figure in the distance
pulling a lever which let loose a deluge of brown liquid. He had a
portly physique. He stood in the shadows, slouched. When I
approached him, he turned his head to look at me. We locked eyes. It
felt as though a jolt of electricity was running through my entire body.
I recognized this face. It was such a shock that it took me a few
seconds to get my bearings. This face was so familiar to me...and my
reaction was so intensely physical.

"Jim E.?" The words came out of his mouth in an extremely high-
pitched whisper.

"My god, is that you Mark F.?"

We immediately embraced. His obese body was soft and comfortable
to press up against. My brother looked like he had aged 40 years since
I last saw him. He looked like a 60-year-old man. But the truth is he
was only 22.

Mark F. never suffered from degenerative disorders the way I did.
But I suppose the trauma of living at Shacklebury Heights had aged

him prematurely.

"What the hell are you doing here at the B&M Factory?" I asked.

"Headmaster Withersby at Shacklebury Heights, he owns this factory. He forces a lot of the boys from the school to work here."

"And he's paying you well, I hope?"

"No, we work making the canned bread in exchange for room and board at Schaklebury Heights."

"That's absurd!" I yelled. "Let's get you out of here! Now!"

"Absolutely not, Jim E. I like my life here. I'm happier than I've ever been. Headmaster Withersby has taught me valuable life lessons which I'll never forget. I've truly discovered myself and thank God that Mum sent me to Shacklebury Heights!" He pulled a lever and brown liquid splooged out of an industrial tube.

"Thanks for visiting, Jim E. It was nice to see you. But Headmaster Withersby doesn't approve of visitors. So, it would be best if you left."

This poor bastard had a bad case of Stockholm Syndrome. There was nothing I could do about it. I walked out of the B&M Canning factory feeling bittersweet. It was wonderful to hug and grapple the flesh of my older brother, but it was sad that he was doomed to a life of indentured servitude.

It was a lot to process and I needed a drink. I bought a large case of Bud Light, drank 19 of them and went to bed in my hotel room. Woke up the next morning and took an Uber to the airport.

Things at the airport were odd. People were wearing surgical masks and acting funny. Apparently, a brand-new disease which they called the Coranavirus was circling around the world and infecting people left and right.

I flew back to Manchester with a new outlook on life. I had changed. But so, had the world. I was being told to stand 6 feet apart from others and that many old folks would be dropping dead soon.

 When I arrived at my flat I walked in on something I had hoped never to see. Mum was seated on the couch and she was being fingered by that nefarious Smothfeld. I became enraged at the site of this.

"You've betrayed my Father!" I screamed.

"Everyone needs love, Jim!" Mum said. "I don't question your relationship with Mildred after all!"

"Where in fuck's sake is Mildred?" I asked.

"She never returned from work" said Mum. It was 8 pm. Mildred was always home by 5:08. At that precise moment the phone rang.

It was a doctor from Withington Community Hospital calling to let me know that Mildred had been in a car crash. Her car was hit by a Freight Truck on the M60.

She had flown through the windshield and landed, very auspiciously, on an abandoned mattress on the side of the road. Landing on the mattress saved her life initially, but it was a very bouncy and springy mattress.

Her body bounced off the mattress and back into the highway where her skull was crushed into bits by the wheel of the very same freight truck.

She was taken to Withington where doctors attempted to glue her brain and skull back together, but to no avail. It had been smashed up into too many bits.

I began to cry uncontrollably.

"What's wrong Jim?" said Mum.

"Fuck off!" I screamed. "I'm going to live with Aunt Melba May at her cottage!"

10. Aunt Melba May's Cottage And My Career In Music

I've always been fond of my Aunt Melba May. She lives in a cottage near Knutsford, just outside of Manchester. She agreed to take me in once I told her about the conflicts I was having with Mum. Aunt Melba May is my Father's sister and she's always taken umbrage with my Mum. Melba May relishes any opportunity to disparage Mum. So, boarding with yours truly would afford her 24/7 opportunity to shit talk with abandon.

I told Melba about Smothfeld fingering Mum and we mutually retched. Melba helped me recover from the death of Mildred. She would bring cans of bread to my bed every afternoon and made Red Bull Vodkas for me in the evening. Her Red Bull Vodkas were almost as good as the ones at Ye Olde Cock!

Staying in the country was a change of pace for a city boy like me, but I liked it. I decided I wanted to record an album to reflect on all of the things that have happened in my life. From peas to unrequited love, I had a lot to say as singer-songwriter. So, I went about recording an album.

The album was recorded in the basement of my Aunt Melba May's cottage using Garage Band on my iPad, which I received as a Christmas present from Aunt Melba May. I was inspired by the pastoral ambience that Aunt Melba May's Cottage had to offer. The colours are vivid and delightful. I appreciate all that that woman has done for me, although she can be rather insufferable. Much like my Mother she has a penchant for making peas. I don't like the taste of Peas. Additionally, she cries all the time and her tears smell like shit! I also cry very regularly and I've discovered that my tears also taste like shit so I cannot hold it against her...but other people's smelly tears are always more offensive than one's one.

As I'm not versed in any musical instrumentation I hired some local lads who are in a pretty cool band in Knutsford called The Ivy League. They recorded the instrumentation with my guidance. Of course, we followed Covid regulations and wore masks and stayed well over 6 feet apart during the recording process. Additionally, we had plenty of hand sanitizer at our disposal which I used to wipe down the microphones I was using as I have a tendency to get rather loud and passionate while singing. The Ivy League were very generous with their time and only charged me £4,000 to do all the music for the album. They asked me not to name them because they were embarrassed by both the music and the lyrics.

Aunt Melba lent me the money to have this album Mixed and Mastered by a fellow who asked that I not use his name publicly, as he wasn't fond of the music on the album either. I hired him on the website Fiverr.com. It cost £50 pounds and it was worth every penny.

Then I uploaded the album to Bandcamp. I decided to call it *Jim E. Brown Sings His Love Songs*

All this album business happened in the last two months. I've got a lot more life to live, even with my degenerative conditions. And I've left out a lot of juicy stories and occurrences. But I figure that 40 some pages is enough for now as an introduction to how I became me. Thanks for reading the first installment of my memoirs.

ABOUT THE AUTHOR

Poet and Artist/Activist Jim E. Brown's was born in Manchester on September 10, 2001 just one day before the 911.

He is an alcoholic and has several degenerative conditions.

In 2021 he released his debut album, *Jim E. Brown Sings His Love Songs*.